Writing Skills
2

Diana Hanbury King

Educators Publishing Service, Inc.
Cambridge and Toronto

OTHER BOOKS BY DIANA HANBURY KING

Writing Skills for the Adolescent
Cursive Writing Skills
Keyboarding Skills
Writing Skills 1

Educators Publishing Service, Inc.
31 Smith Place, Cambridge, Massachusetts 02138

ISBN 0-8388-2051-4

July, 1996 Printing

CONTENTS

TO THE TEACHER

Learning to write well is one of the most important skills students can acquire. Fortunately, with the right kind of practice, it is a skill that *can* be learned. The exercises in *Writing Skills 2* are designed to provide this practice. By working with this material, students can improve their knowledge of sentence structure and learn some of the more common patterns of expository writing. Above all, they will gain confidence.

The grammar introduced has been kept simple and straightforward and is presented in conjunction with writing sentences. Students practice combining various elements in order to compose interesting and varied sentences. Writing sentences is good practice; often when engaged in composition and absorbed in their thoughts, students are unable to focus on sentence structure. For those who need more practice in writing, a sentence is a good beginning unit.

While any English curriculum should include creative, narrative, and imaginative writing in all its forms, success in subject matter courses is dependent on the ability to organize and support ideas—the essence of expository writing. *Writing Skills 2* introduces expository writing in a careful step-by-step fashion. The model paragraphs are written in language that can be emulated by students, and the topics and suggested writing assignments are taken from situations with which they are likely to be familiar. The progression is from the basic paragraph (usually five sentences) to the lengthier expanded paragraph, and culminates in the five-paragraph essay. The types of paragraphs introduced begin with the simple example paragraph and progress to the more complex comparison and contrast paragraph. At any stage, students can begin to apply the skills they have learned to writing about the literature they read and the social studies and science they study.

An important by-product of learning expository writing is improved reading comprehension. As students learn to organize their ideas in certain patterns, they will become increasingly aware of what the writers they read are trying to do. This is particularly the case with textbooks, where students often have difficulty in distinguishing between main ideas and supporting details.

The exercises in *Writing Skills 2* can be used as small group or classroom activities. However, the directions and examples are clear enough that some students will be able to progress through the text independently, or with only a modicum of guidance.

Writing Skills for the Adolescent contains many exercises to supplement those in this book and should be used as a teacher's guide.

NOUNS

Developing better writing skills depends on learning to write better sentences. The exercises in this book are designed to help you structure interesting and varied sentences.

A complete **sentence** expresses a single idea. It must have a subject (noun or pronoun) and a verb. Usually the subject comes at or near the beginning of a sentence.

A **noun** is the name of a person, place, or thing. Use each of the following nouns as the subject of a sentence.

airport   skyscraper   sunflowers   engineer   telescope

magazines   peninsula   dolphin   California   chocolate

1. _____

2. _____

3. _____

4. _____

5. _____

6. _____

7. _____

8. _____

9. _____

10. _____

An **abstract noun** is the name of a quality or idea. Use each of the following abstract nouns as the subject of a sentence.

health   emergency   courage   peace   secrets

1. _____

2. _____

3. _____

4. _____

5. _____

PRONOUNS

A **pronoun** takes the place of a noun. On a separate sheet of paper write sentences using each of the following pronouns as the subject.

I   he   who   it   anybody

we   she   they   you   nothing

VERBS

A **verb** is usually an action word. One way to test whether or not a word is a verb is by seeing if it will fit into the following pattern:

I **talk**	We **talk**
You **talk**	You (plural) **talk**
He/she/it **talks**	They **talk**

On a separate sheet of paper use the following verbs in sentences. You may add endings such as *-ed*, *-ing*, or *-s* and/or helping verbs such as *am, is, was, will, shall, have, has,* or *had.*

invent   travel   accept   paint   vanish

complain   insist   organize   intervene   decrease

Beginning sentences with words like the ones below will help you write more interesting, varied sentences. Write sentences that begin with each of the following words.

1. Silently _____

2. Beyond _____

3. Intentionally _____

4. Yesterday _____

5. Avoiding _____

6. Unless _____

7. As soon as _____

8. Above _____

9. Whenever _____

10. Fortunately _____

FOUR KINDS OF SENTENCES

There are four kinds of sentences.

- Statements (also called declarative sentences)
- Questions (also called interrogative sentences)
- Exclamations (also called exclamatory sentences)
- Commands (also called imperative sentences)

Most sentences are **statements**, which simply give information. Write statements as answers to these questions. Make sure your statements are complete sentences.

1. What don't they like about it?

   _____

2. What is dangerous about it?

   _____

3. How will I recognize you?

   _____

4. Do they know what they are doing?

   _____

5. Where did she hide the key?

   _____

Now write questions to go with these answers.

1. _____

   He doesn't have enough money.

2. _____

   You need a tent and a sleeping bag.

3. _____

   It can't weigh more than forty pounds.

4. _____

   I bought it a year ago, but it was not new then.

5. _____

   I refuse to answer such a stupid question.

EXCLAMATIONS AND COMMANDS

Exclamations are used to communicate urgency or strong emotion. Study the following sets of examples.

Don't go near the edge!　　Watch out! It's coming towards us.
That paint is wet!　　Oh no! We missed the last bus.
Take that snake away!　　Ouch! That hurts.
Now you've broken it!　　Wonderful! We'll be there.

Now write five exclamations of each type. For the second type, you can use these expressions, called interjections.

Stop!　　Great!　　Help!　　Quick!　　Yuck!　　Oops!

1. _____

2. _____

3. _____

4. _____

5. _____

6. _____

7. _____

8. _____

9. _____

10. _____

Commands begin with a verb. The subject is always *you* and is generally omitted. Study these examples; then write six of your own.

Take me to your leader.　　Change the oil.
Drive carefully.　　Be here by six o'clock.
Please set the table.　　Please don't feed the bears.

1. _____

2. _____

3. _____

4. _____

5. _____

6. _____

4

FOUR KINDS OF SENTENCES

Review the four kinds of sentences by writing one of each type for every noun and verb on this page. The first one has been done for you.

1. bus

   The bus leaves at four-thirty.

   What time does the bus leave?

   Hurry! The bus is leaving now.

   Take the next bus to Riverdale.

2. tiger

   _____

   _____

   _____

   _____

3. canoe

   _____

   _____

   _____

   _____

4. drive

   _____

   _____

   _____

   _____

On a separate sheet of paper continue this exercise using the following nouns and verbs.

time	New York	whale	refuse	look
departure	study	Jose	capture	imagine

LISTS

When you write you need lots of ideas. Making lists is a good way to practice generating ideas. Try to think of ten items for each of these headings.

1. Vehicles

_____

_____

_____

_____

_____

_____

_____

_____

_____

_____

2. Dangerous jobs

_____

_____

_____

_____

_____

_____

_____

_____

_____

_____

3. Rock groups

_____

_____

_____

_____

_____

_____

_____

_____

_____

_____

4. Geographic features

_____

_____

_____

_____

_____

_____

_____

_____

_____

_____

LISTS

Use some of the headings below to make lists on separate sheets of paper. Try to think of fifteen items for each. Do one a day for a while.

1. things in your basement
2. shiny things
3. uses for milk cartons
4. airlines
5. triangular things
6. colors
7. sources of protein
8. street signs
9. words that go together (pen and ink)
10. mythical beasts
11. choices (black or white)
12. American authors
13. things you could bet on
14. loud noises
15. uses for a computer
16. lakes
17. things that change color
18. similes
19. useless inventions
20. kinds of rock
21. things not to touch
22. things that itch
23. causes of pollution
24. costumes
25. books you would recommend
26. wars
27. things you can do in 5 minutes
28. formulae
29. sources of light
30. liquids
31. things to make lists of
32. weekly magazines
33. things that are free
34. tools
35. words that alliterate
36. dances
37. kinds of weather
38. uses for a brick
39. events at a county fair
40. colleges
41. reference books
42. newspapers
43. North American wild animals
44. sauces
45. construction materials
46. cartoon strips
47. things you have to have a ticket for
48. things we import
49. things to keep in a wallet
50. emotions

Write headings for the lists below.

1. _____

sneakers
hiking boots
slippers
loafers
dancing shoes

2. _____

bus
train
streetcar
subway
trolley bus

3. _____

radio
telephone
fax machine
mail
telegram

4. _____

hooks and eyes
laces
buttons
zippers
snaps

7

SUPPORTING SENTENCES

Write complete sentences for the lists below. These sentences are called **supporting sentences** because they support the heading. The first one has been done for you.

1. Ways I have of relaxing

   I take a hot shower.

   I listen to music.

   I watch television.

   I read a magazine.

   I go for a walk alone.

2. Things I do on weekends

   _____

   _____

   _____

   _____

   _____

3. Excuses for being late

   _____

   _____

   _____

   _____

   _____

4. Safety precautions for swimmers

   _____

   _____

   _____

   _____

   _____

Mark your best set of sentences with an asterisk.

TOPIC SENTENCES

Writing paragraphs is quite similar to writing lists. Headings like the ones you used for lists are called topic sentences when they are used for paragraphs. A **topic sentence** gives the main idea of a paragraph. In these exercises, read the topic sentence and write supporting sentences just as you did on the previous page. The first set has been done for you.

1. Many things can go wrong with a car.

   You can run out of oil.

   You can have a flat tire.

   You can have a dead battery.

2. You have to take care of a bicycle.

   _____

   _____

   _____

3. I would like to change several things about my school.

   _____

   _____

   _____

4. I would like to learn to do several things.

   _____

   _____

   _____

5. A number of things can go wrong with a house.

   _____

   _____

   _____

6. I have several suggestions for the president.

   _____

   _____

   _____

CONCLUDING SENTENCES

A **concluding sentence** is a final sentence that sums up a paragraph and tells the reader that you have finished your discussion. There are often several possibilities for the concluding sentence. Write three supporting sentences for each topic sentence. Then add a concluding sentence. The first one has been done for you.

1. I have several ways of saving money.

   I walk instead of riding a bus.

   I take sandwiches instead of buying lunch.

   I write letters instead of phoning long distance.

   C.S. *I prefer saving to asking my parents for more money.*

2. I know several ways of finding a job.

   _____

   _____

   _____

   C.S. _____

3. Traveling by bus has some disadvantages.

   _____

   _____

   _____

   C.S. _____

4. I enjoy visiting malls for several reasons.

   _____

   _____

   _____

   C.S. _____

5. There are some things I am too old to do.

   _____

   _____

   _____

   C.S. _____

ORGANIZING A PARAGRAPH

A **basic paragraph** consists of a topic sentence, at least three supporting sentences, and a concluding sentence. You are ready to organize some basic paragraphs. Write a set of sentences for each of these titles.

My Responsibilities at Home

T.S. _____

1. _____

2. _____

3. _____

C.S. _____

Popular Hobbies

T.S. _____

1. _____

2. _____

3. _____

C.S. _____

Things That Annoy Me

T.S. _____

1. _____

2. _____

3. _____

C.S. _____

Study the format of the paragraph below. Notice that the title is centered and that the first word is indented.

Saving Money

I have several ways of saving money. I walk instead of riding a bus. I take sandwiches instead of buying lunch. I write letters instead of talking on the phone long distance. I prefer saving to asking my parents for more money.

BASIC PARAGRAPHS

When you write a paragraph, do not underline the title. Center it and capitalize the first word and all the important words. Skip a line after the title, and indent the beginning of your paragraph. Write basic paragraphs for three of the following titles. You can write additional ones on separate sheets of paper.

New Movies   Making Pottery   The Telephone   Trains
My Room   The Cafeteria   Newspapers   Ice

_____

_____

_____

_____

_____

_____

_____

_____

_____

_____

_____

_____

_____

_____

_____

_____

_____

_____

ADJECTIVES

Adjectives describe nouns; they tell more about them. Draw arrows from the adjective(s) to the nouns they describe. The first two have been done for you.

wild horses

heavy traffic

silent night

insulting remark

dangerous situation

azure skies

soft, powdery snow

shy child

wounded veteran

interesting question

sudden, loud noise

deep, dark forest

jagged peaks

wise decision

large diamond ring

famous ancestor

electric blanket

long and perilous journey

astute lawyer

random selection

ridiculous suggestion

illegal act

Fill in the blanks with adjectives. Draw arrows.

1. _____ person

3. _____ assignment

5. _____ idea

7. _____ navy

9. _____ doctor

2. _____ weapon

4. _____ canyon

6. _____ action

8. _____ shadow

10. _____ skateboard

Fill in the blanks with nouns. Draw arrows.

1. durable _____

3. adequate _____

5. insoluble _____

7. complicated _____

9. shining _____

2. edible _____

4. vast _____

6. delicate _____

8. unfriendly _____

10. impossible _____

On a separate sheet of paper write five sentences using any of the phrases you wrote above.

ADJECTIVES

Rewrite, changing the adjective.

Rewrite, changing the noun.

1. deep water

   cool water
   _____

   _____

   _____

   _____

2. deep water

   deep trouble
   _____

   _____

   _____

   _____

3. warm clothes

   _____

   _____

   _____

   _____

4. warm clothes

   _____

   _____

   _____

   _____

5. important reason

   _____

   _____

   _____

   _____

6. important reason

   _____

   _____

   _____

   _____

7. nuclear energy

   _____

   _____

   _____

   _____

8. nuclear energy

   _____

   _____

   _____

   _____

9. modern house

   _____

   _____

   _____

   _____

10. modern house

    _____

    _____

    _____

    _____

ADVERBS

Adverbs describe verbs; they tell when, where, or how something happens. They generally come after the verb and often (but not always) end in *-ly*. Draw arrows from the adverbs to the verbs they describe. The first one has been done for you.

coming soon

contributed generously

lived underground

folded neatly

answered angrily

pay promptly today

misinform deliberately

fought long and hard

went away happily

spoke wisely and well

surrender unconditionally

changed significantly

travels abroad now

swayed perilously

went forth boldly

observes carefully

stopped abruptly

accept gratefully

injure seriously

dressed slowly and carefully

From the list above, select two adverbs for each category.

adverbs that tell how _____   _____

adverbs that tell where _____   _____

adverbs that tell when _____   _____

Fill in the blanks with adverbs. Draw arrows.

1. jump _____   2. spoke _____

3. eats _____   4. danced _____

5. paint _____   6. swims _____

7. decide _____   8. identify _____

Fill in the blanks with verbs. Draw arrows.

1. _____ late   2. _____ brightly

3. _____ solidly   4. _____ instantly

5. _____ next   6. _____ westward

7. _____ alone   8. _____ peacefully

ADVERBS

Rewrite, changing the adverb.

1. gave away

   gave generously
   _____

   _____

   _____

   _____

3. uses wisely

   _____

   _____

   _____

   _____

5. drive carefully

   _____

   _____

   _____

   _____

7. arrived first

   _____

   _____

   _____

   _____

9. moved forward

   _____

   _____

   _____

   _____

Rewrite, changing the verb.

2. gave away

   walked away
   _____

   _____

   _____

   _____

4. uses wisely

   _____

   _____

   _____

   _____

6. drive carefully

   _____

   _____

   _____

   _____

8. arrived first

   _____

   _____

   _____

   _____

10. moved forward

   _____

   _____

   _____

   _____

BASIC PARAGRAPHS

Write three basic paragraphs. Remember that you need a topic sentence, three supporting sentences, and a concluding sentence. Choose your own titles, or select from this list.

Useful Trees   Popular Fads
Careless Habits   Quick Meals
Advantages of City Life   How I Get My Exercise

_____

_____

_____

_____

_____

_____

_____

_____

_____

_____

_____

_____

_____

_____

_____

_____

_____

_____

COMPOUND SENTENCES

A compound word like *basketball* is made of two separate words that can stand alone. A **compound sentence** is similar. It is made of two separate sentences, and each one can stand alone. The two parts are joined with words called **coordinating conjunctions**, such as *and*, *but*, *or*, *nor*,* *for* (meaning "because"), and *yet*. Try to memorize this list.

Write some compound sentences by following the patterns below. Underline each conjunction and make sure that it is preceded by a comma.

1. The sun was shining brightly, **and** there was not a cloud in the sky.

    _____

    _____

2. His parents seem strict, **but** they let him stay out all night.

    _____

    _____

3. Their telephone is out of order, **or** they have gone away for the weekend.

    _____

    _____

4. She didn't have time to do her homework, **nor** could she practice her violin.

    _____

    _____

5. I need to go to the bank, **for** I have no money left in my wallet.

    _____

    _____

6. Some people say they care about pollution, **yet** they don't even bother to recycle newspapers and bottles.

    _____

    _____

On separate sheets of paper, write compound sentences for the nouns and verbs on the first two pages of this book.

*Notice that if you use *nor*, the word order after *nor* changes. For example, The law was never enforced, **nor** was it repealed.

COMPOUND SENTENCES

Another way of constructing a compound sentence is to connect both parts of the sentence with a semicolon. Study these examples; then write five compound sentences of your own.

Baby birds are helpless; they depend on their parents for food.
I don't want to stay in this motel; it doesn't have a swimming pool.
The service there is terrible; they never bother to clean the windshield.

1. _____
2. _____
3. _____
4. _____
5. _____

RUN-ON SENTENCES

A run-on sentence is a type of sentence error that students sometimes make. A **run-on sentence** has two main clauses, or sentences, that run together with no conjunction or semicolon separating the two parts. Read the following run-on sentences.

I miss my friends they have all gone away for the summer.
Lightning struck the pole all the lights in the house went out.
They would like to go to Hawaii they cannot afford it.

There are three ways of fixing run-on sentences. You will learn two of them now.

• You can make two sentences.

I miss my friends. They have all gone away for the summer.
Lightning struck the pole. All the lights in the house went out.
They would like to go to Hawaii. They cannot afford it.

Although these sentences are correct, you may end up with too many short sentences.

• A better way of fixing a run-on sentence is to turn it into a compound sentence by using a semicolon or by using a coordinating conjunction preceded by a comma.

I miss my friends; they have all gone away for the summer.
Lightning struck the pole, and all the lights in the house went out.
They would like to go to Hawaii, but they cannot afford it.

RUN-ON SENTENCES

Correct these run-on sentences by turning them into compound sentences. Insert either a semicolon or a coordinating conjunction (*and*, *but*, *or*, *nor*, *for*, or *yet*). Choose the coordinating conjunction that best shows the relationship between the two clauses.

1. The earthquake was a terrible disaster thousands of people were left homeless.

   _____

2. She always washes the car, her brother takes care of the lawn.

   _____

3. It was my first date I was very nervous.

   _____

4. The car won't start we had better take the bus.

   _____

5. I have a new bicycle something is wrong with the gears.

   _____

6. There may be life in outer space my science teacher doesn't believe there is.

   _____

7. I was sure our team would win, the game ended in a tie.

   _____

8. The dog got into the trash can again, garbage is scattered all over the yard.

   _____

Being able to identify run-on sentences is important so that you can eliminate them from your writing. Write three run-on sentences below to show that you understand what they are. Then correct each one in the best way possible.

1. _____

   _____

2. _____

   _____

3. _____

   _____

PREPOSITIONAL PHRASES

A **prepositional phrase** is a group of words that begins with a preposition and ends with a noun or pronoun. A phrase does not have a subject or a verb. You will find a list of common prepositions inside the front cover of this book.

You can use phrases instead of adjectives or adverbs to describe nouns and verbs. Place parentheses around each phrase, and draw an arrow to the noun or verb it describes. The first one has been done for you.

1. the sign (on the tree)

2. carved with a chisel

3. picture on the wall

4. dreamed about a ship

5. worked below the ground

6. grew in the park

Add a noun to each phrase below.

1. _____ under the table

2. _____ in the water

3. _____ of the committee

4. _____ from a stranger

Add a verb to each phrase below.

1. _____ through town

2. _____ across the bay

3. _____ before breakfast

4. _____ during recess

On a separate sheet of paper write the following words and add a prepositional phrase to describe each one.

Nouns: cat, boat, appointment, movie, journey, history.
Verbs: go, supplied, works, mail, talking, demonstrate.

Notice that you can use more than one prepositional phrase in a sentence.

a piece (of chalk) (on the floor)
dishes (in the cabinet) (above the sink)
watchman (at the gate) (of the city)

sat (by the fire) (in silence)
called (for help) (in vain)
went (to college) (for four years)

A combination of an adjective and a prepositional phrase can describe a noun.

a broken pencil (without an eraser)

A combination of an adverb and a prepositional phrase can describe a verb.

walked slowly (on crutches)

On a separate sheet of paper write five nouns described by a combination of adjectives and prepositional phrases and five verbs described by a combination of adverbs and prepositional phrases.

PREPOSITIONAL PHRASES

Prepositional phrases that describe nouns are called **adjective phrases,** and those that describe verbs are called **adverb phrases.** Place the prepositional phrases in parentheses and label each *adj.* or *adv.* according to its function. The first one has been done for you.

<u>*adv.*</u> 1. stayed (on the track)　　　　　_____ 2. surge of energy

_____ 3. life on the island　　　　　_____ 4. released from jail

_____ 5. covered with snow　　　　　_____ 6. acquisition of wealth

_____ 7. conversation at lunch　　　　　_____ 8. supervise with care

Use any five of the phrases in sentences.

1. _____

2. _____

3. _____

4. _____

5. _____

In the following sentences, cross out all the prepositional phrases and write what is left of each sentence in the space below. Notice that you can eliminate all prepositional phrases (as well as adjectives and adverbs) and still have a complete sentence.

1. At ten o'clock in the morning, we heard a knock on the door.

_____

2. The children loved to play in the sand at the beach.

_____

3. The keys to the boat fell into the lake.

_____

4. Our friends stopped by the house on their way to the movies.

_____

5. Deforestation of the Amazon Basin and depletion of the ozone layer are serious ecological concerns.

_____

EXPANDED PARAGRAPHS

An **expanded paragraph** is a full-length paragraph that enables you to give as much information as you like about each one of your supporting ideas. To make your meaning clear you need to separate your supporting ideas with transitions. A **transition** gives the reader a signal that you have finished discussing one idea and are preparing to go on to the next. The following are the most common transitions:

first	second	last
in the first place	next	finally

The following topic is developed first as a basic paragraph and then as an expanded paragraph.

Problems with Planet Earth

Humans are doing several things that are seriously damaging the planet on which we live. We are destroying the forests and the wildlife. We are polluting the atmosphere and the oceans. We are heating up the earth. We need to act now to repair the damage that has already been done and to prevent further damage in the future.

Problems with Planet Earth

Human beings are doing several things that are seriously damaging the planet on which we live. First, we are destroying the forests for their lumber. We are also burning forests in order to create more grazing land. The destruction of tropical forests is particularly serious as they provide the habitat for at least half the plant and animal species in the world. Once a plant or an animal is extinct, there is no bringing it back. Next, we are polluting the air, the earth, and the waters. Smokestacks from factories pour gases into the air. Millions of cars contribute to smog all over the industrialized world. Lakes and rivers have been polluted with industrial wastes, pesticides, and acid rain. Garbage of every kind has been dumped in the ocean and is even beginning to wash up on the beaches. The soil has been damaged with pesticides and nuclear wastes. Last, we are heating up the world. The gases we are putting into the atmosphere result in what is called the greenhouse effect. Deforestation and desertification also contribute to making the earth warmer. We must take immediate action if we are to repair the damage we have already done and prevent further damage.

Find and circle the three transitions in the expanded paragraph.

Select two of the basic paragraphs you have already written and develop them into expanded paragraphs on separate sheets of paper. When you have finished, find and circle your transitions. Each one should be followed by a comma.

KINDS OF PARAGRAPHS

Now that you have practiced writing both basic and expanded paragraphs, you are ready to learn to write different kinds of expository paragraphs. An **expository paragraph** is a paragraph that explains something. It differs from both narrative writing, which tells a story, and from descriptive writing, which describes something. Expository writing is the kind of writing that you will be expected to do most often in school and college. For that reason, it is important to learn to do it well. Six types of expository paragraphs are introduced in this book, as follows:

- Example paragraph
- Reason paragraph
- Definition paragraph
- Process paragraph
- Classification paragraph
- Comparison and contrast paragraph

Understanding that there are different kinds of paragraphs will help more than your writing ability—it will improve your reading comprehension, particularly when it comes to textbooks. You will be better able to understand how writers organize their thoughts. Take the time to learn each type thoroughly. Practice writing basic paragraphs and then expanded paragraphs in each category. As you write, increase your command of transitions.

An **example paragraph** uses examples for supporting ideas. If you were writing about famous people or interesting places in your town, you would support your topic sentence with examples.

A **process paragraph** explains how to do something step by step. If you wanted to write about making a bookshelf or a pizza, you would write a process paragraph.

A **reason paragraph** uses reasons for supporting ideas. You would write a reason paragraph if you wanted to explain why people should not start smoking or why your student government wants to raise money.

A **classification paragraph** classifies, or divides things into groups. You could divide people into men and women, young and old, or working and unemployed. You could divide the world into climatic zones or fish into saltwater species and freshwater species.

A **definition paragraph** defines something. You would write a definition paragraph if you wanted to define democracy, poverty, or success.

A **comparison and contrast paragraph** compares and contrasts two things, such as two restaurants or two schools.

List the six types of expository paragraphs introduced in this book.

1. _____   2. _____

3. _____   4. _____

5. _____   6. _____

EXAMPLE PARAGRAPHS

An **example paragraph** gives examples. In a basic example paragraph each one of the supporting sentences gives a different example.

Helping the Environment

There are several ways in which you can help the environment. You can avoid waste by recycling. You can avoid polluting. You can plant trees. These are simple things, but they do make a difference.

Boring

All of us have to do some boring things in our daily lives. We have to get dressed and make our beds in the morning. We have to do household tasks such as setting tables and doing dishes. We have to listen to conversations in which we have no interest. There is really no way of avoiding some boredom in our lives unless we can retreat into the world of our imagination.

In the paragraphs above, underline the topic sentence and the conclusion. Each paragraph has three supporting sentences. You need at least three, but you can certainly have more.

Write an example paragraph below. Choose from these titles or invent your own.

Having Fun on the Boardwalk   Rules I Could Do Without
Things People Collect   Common Misconceptions
Forms of Communication   Television Commercials

_____

_____

_____

_____

_____

_____

_____

_____

_____

Write another basic example paragraph on a separate sheet of paper.

EXAMPLE PARAGRAPHS

You can easily change any basic example paragraph into an expanded example paragraph. Use the transitions you have already learned to separate your supporting ideas, each one of which will be a new example, or use the following transitions:

for example	for instance
the first/second/third example	the first/second/third instance
another example	yet another example
the last example	the final example

The basic paragraph about ways of helping the environment has been expanded below to give more information about each one of the examples.

Helping the Environment

Each of us can help the environment in several ways. For example, recycling can cut down on waste. Wherever you live, find out about recycling. In many states, grocery stores will recycle bottles. Many towns have recycling centers to which you can take newspapers as well as bottles. Never throw anything away that someone else could use. Give used clothing to local charities. Find out what to do with furniture your family no longer needs; having a small yard sale is better than throwing things away. Another way in which we can help the environment is by not polluting. Never pour the water or turpentine in which you have cleaned a paint brush onto the ground. Swat flies or use flypaper instead of spraying. Finally, you can plant trees. Oak trees live for a long time and can be started from acorns that you gather in the fall. Often the U.S. Forest Service will sell seedlings very inexpensively. Contact organizations such as the scouts and the Sierra Club to find out about their tree-planting programs. These are just a few simple examples of what we can do, but they really make a difference.

On a separate sheet of paper, expand one of the basic example paragraphs that you have already written.

Then write two more example paragraphs, one basic and one expanded. Choose from these topic sentences, or invent your own.

Some accidents are the result of carelessness.
Our neighborhood has some interesting places.
I have learned several things from my friends.
On long car journeys you can play various games.
The apartment needs some repair work.
Some advertisements are misleading.

PROCESS PARAGRAPHS

A **process paragraph** tells how to do something step by step. You should arrange your steps in time order. For example, your first step might be to collect everything you need. If there are more than three steps, you will need more than three supporting ideas. Always begin with a topic sentence and end with a conclusion. The following are examples of basic process paragraphs.

Setting Up a Campsite

Setting up a campsite is a lot of work. You have to pitch your tent in the right place. You have to build a campfire. You have to find a water supply. You have to dig a latrine. If you do all this work properly, you will be able to camp in comfort for several days.

Bean Soups

Soups made from dried beans make an excellent lunch or supper dish. Soak the beans for several hours. Fry some onions and green peppers. Add them to the beans, together with a can of tomatoes and some water or chicken stock. Cook over a low flame for several hours. Serve with rice, bread and butter, and perhaps a green salad. This is a meal everyone enjoys.

Write a basic process paragraph. Invent your own topic, or write about one of these.

Packing for a Weekend Trip   Setting Up an Aquarium
Making a Model   Planting a Garden

_____

_____

_____

_____

_____

_____

_____

_____

_____

PROCESS PARAGRAPHS

When you write an expanded process paragraph, you may want to use some of these transitions.

to begin with	then
the first/second/third step	also
at this point	when
next	the final/last step
finally	at last

Here is the paragraph about setting up a campsite expanded into a full-length process paragraph.

Setting Up a Campsite

Setting up a campsite properly involves a lot of work. First of all, you have to find a good place to pitch your tent. You need level ground free of rocks. Select a fairly high spot, particularly if there is a chance of rain; you do not want to wake up in the middle of the night in a puddle. Face your tent away from the wind. The next step is to find a place for your fire and to gather a supply of wood and kindling. Make your fireplace by digging a circular pit down to mineral soil. Avoid rocks, which may explode when heated, and overhanging branches low enough to catch fire. Your fire should be small. Collect dry sticks, leaves, and dead wood of various sizes and stack the supply in a handy place. Then you need to check out a nearby water supply for bathing and washing. You should not drink water from streams, rivers, or lakes. Unless there is a good spring, you should carry in your drinking water supply. Finally, you should dig a shallow pit to use as a latrine. Select a site for this at least thirty feet from any stream or other water source. If you do all this work properly, you will be able to camp in comfort for several days.

Since a process paragraph involves a number of steps, it is a good idea to make a list of the steps before you begin writing. If you do this, you are less likely to omit a step.

On a separate sheet of paper write an expanded process paragraph. Expand a basic paragraph you have already written or choose from among these titles.

Making a Rocket	Tacking Up a Horse
Making a Spaghetti Dinner	Skateboarding
Cleaning Up the Basement	Organizing a Bake Sale

Be sure to make a list before you begin.

SUBORDINATE CLAUSES

A **clause** is a group of words with a subject and a verb. There are two kinds of clauses—main clauses and subordinate clauses.

A **main clause** can stand alone; it is a complete sentence by itself. Circle the subject and underline the verb in each of the clauses below. Five are main clauses; turn them into sentences by capitalizing the first word and adding a period at the end.

1. geese migrate in the spring and fall
2. after the lights went out
3. several useful things were for sale at the flea market
4. as the newscaster was reading the morning news
5. because she was born on February 29
6. the hikers were trapped in an unexpected snowstorm
7. although they have an excellent reputation
8. until they can fix the sprinkler system
9. Marie Curie discovered radium
10. even if the package arrives by Wednesday
11. as soon as the plane landed
12. Leonardo da Vinci was left-handed

The second kind of clause is a **subordinate clause.** Since it is not a complete sentence, it cannot stand alone. Subordinate clauses begin with words called subordinating conjunctions.

Subordinating conjunctions connect the two parts of a sentence by telling how, when, where, or why something happens or by giving reasons or conditions. Read the list of the most common subordinating conjunctions inside the front cover of this book.

Draw a box around the subordinating conjunctions in the subordinate clauses above.

Now write five subordinate clauses below. Begin each clause with a subordinating conjunction; use the list inside the front cover. Do not capitalize the subordinating conjunctions because you are not writing complete sentences. Be sure you have a subject and verb in each clause.

1. _____
2. _____
3. _____
4. _____
5. _____

PHRASES AND CLAUSES

Prepositional phrases may start with some of the same words that are used as subordinating conjunctions, but phrases do not have subjects or verbs. Label the following groups of words *ph* for phrase or *cl* for clause.

_____ 1. after a delicious lunch   _____ 2. after we had eaten lunch

_____ 3. before the homecoming game   _____ 4. before we lost the game

_____ 5. until the mail carrier comes   _____ 6. until next Saturday

_____ 7. since 1984   _____ 8. since she was elected

To turn a subordinate clause into a sentence, complete the thought by adding a main clause. Write the subordinate clauses from above on the lines below, and add a main clause to each. The first one has been done for you.

1. *After we had eaten lunch, we realized our money had been stolen.* _____

2. _____

3. _____

4. _____

A **complex sentence** has one main clause and one subordinate clause. The sentences you have just written and the ones below are complex sentences. In each sentence, circle the subordinating conjunction and underline the main clause.

1. While we waited, we became increasingly impatient.

2. They will survive for a month unless they run out of food.

3. Whenever there is a full moon, I have trouble sleeping.

4. She walked into the restaurant as if she owned the place.

5. Although I am allergic to cats, I have two of them.

6. Put those groceries away wherever you can find room.

7. As soon as I looked at the child, I realized he was ill.

8. Until we had television, we were satisfied with the radio.

9. If you find my wallet, please return it to me.

10. I worked all of June and July so that I could afford to go to the beach in August.

Reread these sentences and mark the ones that have commas with asterisks. Notice that if the subordinate clause comes first, you need a comma.

COMPLEX SENTENCES

Write some complex sentences below. Follow these patterns.

1. They played checkers **while** they waited for the bus to arrive.

_____

_____

2. **If** the referees do not get here soon, we will start the game without them.

_____

_____

3. He kept on fighting **although** he had been wounded.

_____

_____

4. **Until** the advent of the automobile, horses provided the main means of transportation.

_____

_____

5. We sent for help **as soon as** we realized the house was on fire.

_____

_____

Write ten more complex sentences.

1. _____

2. _____

3. _____

4. _____

5. _____

6. _____

7. _____

8. _____

9. _____

10. _____

REASON PARAGRAPHS

A **reason paragraph** gives reasons for something. They can be reasons why you like or dislike something, reasons why you believe or choose to do something, reasons why people do something, or many other things. When you are writing this kind of paragraph, it is better not to begin any of your sentences with *because* as doing so makes it easy to end up with an incomplete sentence, or subordinate clause. The following paragraphs are examples of basic reason paragraphs.

Fast Food

There are several reasons why people eat at fast-food restaurants. The service is so quick that you can be served without even having to get out of your car. The food comes from a clean kitchen and is always fresh. Most people can find something that they want to eat. It is cheap. No wonder there are so many fast-food restaurants.

Don't Litter

People should avoid littering the highways for a variety of reasons. Litter on the highways is unsightly and, as much of it is not biodegradable, it stays there forever. Litter is hazardous; glass can cut tires or start a fire, and a carelessly thrown bottle can cause an accident. In many states, people caught littering can be fined as much as a hundred dollars. People should equip their cars with trash bags that can be taken home or emptied into a container at the next gas station.

Write two basic reason paragraphs. Use a separate sheet of paper for the second one. Choose from among these topics.

Why I Enjoy Television
Why I Play Soccer (Baseball)
Don't Start Smoking
Why I Enjoy Parties

Why I Admire _____
Why I Enjoy My Job
A Good Movie
Why I Dislike Long Car Trips

_____

_____

_____

_____

_____

_____

_____

_____

REASON PARAGRAPHS

Use some of the following transitions to separate your supporting ideas or reasons when you write expanded reason paragraphs.

the first/second/third reason	the main reason
one reason	the most important reason
another reason	the final reason
yet/still another reason	the last reason

Study the following paragraph, which is an expanded version of one of the basic paragraphs on the previous page.

Fast Food

There are several reasons why people eat at fast-food restaurants. The most important reason is that the service is fast. When you go in, rows of people are waiting to take your order and you seldom have to stand in line for more than a couple of minutes. Often there is drive-in service so that you do not even have to get out of the car. This service is a great convenience for a family making a trip with young children. Another reason is that the food is fresh. Chains of fast-food restaurants sell so much food that they have to order fresh food daily. You do not risk getting food poisoning from spoiled food. Yet another reason for the popularity of fast-food restaurants is that the menus have sufficient variety. Depending on what chain you choose, you can have every sort of hamburger, chicken, fish, pizza, or even taco. In addition, some places serve an interesting selection of breakfast foods. Soft drinks, milk, pie, and ice cream are also available. A final reason is that the price is right. Where else can you satisfy a couple of hungry teenagers for under ten dollars? No wonder there are so many fast-food restaurants.

Expand one of your basic reason paragraphs on a separate sheet of paper. Make an outline first to help organize your thoughts.

Title: _____

Topic sentence: _____

First reason: _____

   Details: _____

Second reason: _____

   Details: _____

Third reason: _____

   Details: _____

Conclusion: _____

REASON PARAGRAPHS

In some families both parents work; in others one parent stays home and looks after the home. Write about the advantages or the disadvantages of either situation. An expanded paragraph like this works best if you begin by planning. Make a list of your reasons. Under each reason, list the details that you plan to use and all the information you want to give. Use this outline. If you need more space, use a separate sheet of paper. Remember to start your paragraph with a title.

Reason: _____

    Detail: _____

    Detail: _____

    Detail: _____

Reason: _____

    Detail: _____

    Detail: _____

    Detail: _____

Reason: _____

    Detail: _____

    Detail: _____

    Detail: _____

_____

_____

_____

_____

_____

_____

_____

_____

_____

_____

CLASSIFICATION PARAGRAPHS

The fourth type of paragraph is the **classification paragraph.** In a classification paragraph things are sorted or divided into categories according to some quality they have in common. For instance, library books can be classified as fiction, nonfiction, drama, and poetry. You could also classify books as paperbacks and hardbacks. You must have at least two categories, but you can have more. Your classification paragraph will describe each category and give examples for each.

The following are examples of basic classification paragraphs.

Holidays

There are three kinds of holidays. Holidays such as Christmas and Hanukkah are religious holidays. Other holidays have political or historical significance, such as George Washington's Birthday or July Fourth. There are family holidays such as Mother's Day or birthdays and anniversaries. Because holidays are scattered throughout the year, there is always something to look forward to.

Sports Equipment

Sports can be classified according to the amount of personal equipment that is needed. Some sports, such as jogging or hiking, can be enjoyed with either no equipment or with a single piece of equipment that can be shared by a group. Other sports, such as bicycling, require one or two pieces of equipment. Sports such as skiing require a great deal of elaborate equipment. For some sports, such as yachting, there is no limit to the amount of equipment that can be employed. Fortunately, expensive equipment can usually be rented.

Write two basic classification paragraphs; select from the titles below or choose your own. For some, a basis for classification has been suggested. Write your paragraphs on a separate sheet of paper.

Types of Restaurants (classify according to price)
Breeds of Dogs (classify according to size or use)
Vegetables (classify according to the part of the plant eaten)
Snacks (classify as sweet, sour, salty, and spicy or as nutritious and nonnutritious)
Cars (classify according to size)
Olympic Events
Types of Music

CLASSIFICATION PARAGRAPHS

When you write an expanded classification paragraph, you give detailed information about each category and you provide several examples of each. Useful transitional signals include the following:

the first/the second/the third	another kind
one kind	another type
one type	the last kind
one category	the last type

The following is an example of an expanded classification paragraph.

Holidays

Holidays can be divided into three categories. The first group is that of religious holidays. It is interesting to note that the word *holiday* was originally "holy day," and the first holidays were religious celebrations. In this country we celebrate Christmas and Easter as well as Hanukkah and Rosh Hashanah. Next are holidays for political or historical reasons. These include Thanksgiving, George Washington's Birthday, Lincoln's Birthday, and Independence Day, or Fourth of July. In recent years Martin Luther King's Birthday was added. November 11 was originally dedicated to the memory of those who lost their lives in World War I. Now it honors the dead of all wars, as well as living veterans, and has been renamed Veterans' Day. Labor Day is celebrated on the first Monday in September to honor all workers. Last, there are various family holidays. These include Mother's Day and Father's Day, both of fairly recent origin. Families develop their own ways of celebrating birthdays and anniversaries. On calendars holidays are sometimes marked in red and for this reason are sometimes called red-letter days; because they are scattered throughout the year, there is always something to look forward to.

Underline the transitional expressions in the paragraph above. List the three categories, and give an example of your own for each.

1. _____ Example _____

2. _____ Example _____

3. _____ Example _____

Write another way holidays could be classified.

_____

CLASSIFICATION PARAGRAPHS

There are usually several ways in which something can be classified. For instance, sports can be classified as summer and winter sports, land and water sports, or individual and team sports. List two ways each of the following could be classified.

Fish _____   _____

Toys _____   _____

Houses _____   _____

Fabrics _____   _____

Tools _____   _____

Cities _____   _____

Rocks _____   _____

When you write an expanded classification paragraph, it helps to plan first. Use the outline below to list each category and make a note of the examples you want to use. Use a topic of your own or choose one of the titles suggested on page 35.

Title: _____

First type: _____

    Example: _____

    Example: _____

    Example: _____

Second type: _____

    Example: _____

    Example: _____

    Example: _____

Third type: _____

    Example: _____

    Example: _____

    Example: _____

If you have only two categories, omit the last section. If you need more than three, work on a separate sheet of paper.

After you have completed your outline, write your paragraph on a separate sheet of paper.

ADJECTIVE CLAUSES

Subordinate clauses are of three types: adjective clauses, adverb clauses, and noun clauses.

Adjective clauses are like the adjectives and adjective phrases that you have already studied in this book; they describe nouns and pronouns. However, adjective clauses have a subject and a verb. Adjective clauses usually begin with one of the following words, called relative pronouns: *who, whose, whom, that,* or *which.*

Place parentheses around each of the adjective clauses and draw an arrow to the noun or pronoun it describes. The first one has been done for you.

1. the book (that I lost)
2. anybody who can help us
3. the picture that hung on the wall
4. the person whose car we borrowed
5. people who live in glass houses
6. nobody who is a friend of mine
7. fears that seem irrational
8. the carpenter whom we hired
9. the cat that walked by itself
10. the bed, which was in the corner
11. the doctor whose car broke down
12. those that we liked the best

Now circle the relative pronouns that begin these adjective clauses. Notice that *who, whose,* and *whom* are used for people.

Use any five of the clauses above in sentences. The first one has been done for you.

1. *The book that I lost was found on the bench by the pond.* _____

2. _____

3. _____

4. _____

5. _____

You now know three ways of describing nouns and pronouns.

tree

Adjective: *the tall tree* _____

Adjective phrase: *the tree (on the corner)* _____

Adjective clause: *the tree (that blew down in the night)* _____

NOUN MODIFIERS

Follow the pattern on the previous page by writing an adjective, a phrase, and a clause to describe each noun. Then turn the clause into a complex sentence. The first one has been done for you.

1. mug

   Adjective: _the blue mug_

   Adjective phrase: _the mug (with a chipped rim)_

   Adjective clause: _the mug (that I broke)_

   The mug that I broke did not belong to me.

2. water

   Adjective: _____

   Adjective phrase: _____

   Adjective clause: _____

   _____

3. star

   Adjective: _____

   Adjective phrase: _____

   Adjective clause: _____

   _____

4. watch

   Adjective: _____

   Adjective phrase: _____

   Adjective clause: _____

   _____

Continue this exercise on a separate sheet of paper with the following nouns.

freedom   taxi   paper   storm   raccoon

ADVERB CLAUSES

The second type of subordinate clause is the adverb clause. **Adverb clauses** are like the adverbs and adverb phrases that you have already studied; they describe verbs. Adverb clauses begin with subordinating conjunctions (see the list on the inside front cover of this book). Place parentheses around the adverb clause and draw an arrow to the verb it describes. The first one has been done for you.

1. shopped (because I needed shoes)

2. decided after we had inspected everything

3. walk when it is raining

4. come unless you have another engagement

5. surfs when the waves are high

6. worked although they were exhausted

7. replaced because it was defective

8. married while they were in college

9. looked as if it were hopeless

10. journeyed even though there were dangers

Write adverb clauses to describe these verbs.

skated _____

dance _____

hiking _____

sell _____

delayed _____

served _____

Use some of the groups of words listed above in complex sentences. The first one has been done for you.

1. *Yesterday I shopped because I needed shoes.*

   or *Because I needed shoes, I shopped yesterday.*

2. _____

3. _____

4. _____

5. _____

6. _____

7. _____

8. _____

9. _____

10. _____

VERB MODIFIERS

Add an adverb, a phrase, and a clause to describe each verb; then use the clause in a sentence. The first one has been done for you.

1. come

   Adverb: *come quickly*

   Adverb phrase: *come after the party*

   Adverb clause: *come after the party starts*

   They will come after the party starts.

2. waited

   Adverb: _____

   Adverb phrase: _____

   Adverb clause: _____

   _____

3. talking

   Adverb: _____

   Adverb phrase: _____

   Adverb clause: _____

   _____

4. refuses

   Adverb: _____

   Adverb phrase: _____

   Adverb clause: _____

   _____

5. read

   Adverb: _____

   Adverb phrase: _____

   Adverb clause: _____

   _____

Continue this exercise with the words below on a separate sheet of paper.

leave   hiding   sold   catch   grew

DEFINITION PARAGRAPHS

A **definition paragraph** defines, or gives a definition of, something. Examples are often used to make the meaning clear. There are many different ways of defining things. Study the following basic definition paragraphs.

Windfall Profit

The expression *windfall profit* is commonly used to denote an unexpected profit. Windfalls are apples that fall from trees and can be picked up by anybody, and the expression has come to mean a profit acquired without any particular effort. You could own a piece of property, the value of which increases suddenly. You might go to a flea market and buy an old chair that turns out to be a valuable antique. Windfall profits are mostly the result of luck.

Greenhouse Effect

The greenhouse effect is the name given to the gradual warming of the earth that concerns many environmentalists today. Just as the walls of a greenhouse trap heat, so the blanket of carbon dioxide around the earth traps the radiant heat from the sun. Since the industrial revolution, increasing amounts of carbon dioxide have been released into the atmosphere. Some people think that the excessive heat and drought in the summer of 1988 were caused by the greenhouse effect.

Fads

A fad is something that comes into fashion for a brief period of time and for no particular reason. Toys such as hula hoops have been fads. Jokes, like the knock-knock jokes of the 1960s and expressions like "I dig it" or "What's up?" can become fads. Fashions like the miniskirt or pedal pushers have been fads. Hairstyles such as the beehive and ducktail of the 1950s have been fads. Fads are particularly rife among teenagers, many of whom like to do whatever is the "in" thing.

Write three basic definition paragraphs. Choose from among these topics or select your own. Write your paragraphs on a separate sheet of paper.

Flirting	Selfishness	A Puma
Street Smarts	Integrity	An Idol
First Aid	Tough Love	Stubbornness

DEFINITION PARAGRAPHS

In writing an expanded definition paragraph, you will need to illustrate your definition with examples. You might want to use a comparison, or analogy (as in the paragraph on the greenhouse effect). You may want to discuss the origin of an expression (as in the paragraph on windfall profits). Some of the things you define may have more than one meaning that you will want to explain. Always make your explanation clear by giving specific examples.

The following transitions may be useful.

one meaning	for example
another meaning	an example
for instance	another example

The following is an example of an expanded definition paragraph.

Homesickness

Homesickness is not an illness although it does sound like one. In some ways it is worse than an illness. We usually think of the word in connection with children away from home for the first time, perhaps at a summer camp or at a boarding school. The despair of children in this situation can be very real. The evening, when it starts to get dark, is an especially bad time. Sometimes they will cry themselves to sleep, dream that they are at home, and wake up crying. But homesickness can be experienced by adults as well. For instance, young men and women in the armed forces, away from home and among strangers, often become terribly homesick, as do college students. At that age, the feeling is made worse by embarrassment. They feel like crying, but unlike children, they are unable to do so. People can become homesick when they get married. They have to leave home, often to live in a strange town, away from all their childhood friends. Homesickness is not just missing people; it involves missing places as well. One can feel homesick for a particular house, a village street, a group of trees, a hillside, or a glimpse of the sea beyond the sand dunes. The only way to avoid experiencing homesickness is to live all of one's life in the same place.

Write two expanded definition paragraphs. You can use one of the topics on the previous page, select from this list, or devise your own topics. Work on separate sheets of paper.

Loneliness	Excuses	Morale
Friendship	Greed	Computer Literacy
Prejudice	Adventure	Foolhardiness

COMPARISON AND CONTRAST PARAGRAPHS

The last type of paragraph introduced in this book is the **comparison and contrast paragraph.** This type of paragraph compares and contrasts two things. When you compare things, you describe their similarities; when you contrast things, you describe their differences. There are two ways of organizing such a paragraph. The simplest way is to tell all about one thing and then all about the other. The following two basic comparison and contrast paragraphs do this.

Analog versus* Digital Timepieces

In buying a watch or a clock, you have to decide between digital and analog timepieces. A digital watch has the advantage of greater accuracy. You can tell time to the nearest hundredth of a second. On the other hand, you may find the flashing numbers distracting, and on some watches you have to press a button to see the time. Analog timepieces are generally more attractive in appearance and are in fashion for this reason. They are not as accurate as the digital timepieces, but few of us need to know the time to the exact second anyway. It is, of course, more difficult for a child to learn to tell time with an analog watch or clock. Which do you wear?

Televised versus Live Sports Events

There are two ways of watching sports events; you can go to the games or you can watch them on television. Many major league tickets are expensive—you can pay fifty dollars for a decent seat—and sometimes tickets are unobtainable. If you drive to the game, parking can be a hassle. You can suffer from heat in the summer baseball season and from cold in the winter football season. But there are some advantages. You become part of an audience to a real live game, watching it as it happens with no interruptions. You can yell yourself hoarse when the home team scores. Watching the game on television is certainly cheaper, and you can do it in the comfort of your own living room. You get some wonderful closeup shots, and you get replays in slow motion. Of course, you always wonder what you are missing during those frequent commercial breaks.

Use this pattern of giving all the information about first one and then the other of your items to write two paragraphs on a separate sheet of paper. Select your topics from the following, or devise your own.

Two Friends	Weight Lifting versus Jogging	Radio versus Television
Two Restaurants	City Noises versus Country Noises	How I Have Changed

Versus is a useful word. It means "as opposed to."

44

COMPARISON AND CONTRAST PARAGRAPHS

When you want to compare and contrast something in greater detail, with more likenesses and differences, you need to organize your ideas in a different fashion. You will discuss each point one at a time as it applies to each one of your subjects. The following paragraph makes this clear.

Local Store versus Supermarket

There are a number of differences between my local store and the supermarket in the mall. The first difference is size. My local store is not much bigger than my house. The aisles are narrow, and maneuvering a shopping cart is difficult. The supermarket is huge; it must cover half an acre. The aisles are as wide as a road. Obviously, there is a vast difference in the number of items each can stock. My local store carries only a few brand names of each item, and there are many things that they do not stock at all. My supermarket seems to carry every known brand of toothpaste, cereal, and spaghetti. Furthermore, things are easier to find in my local store. I know where everything is, and I can make a quick tour of the three aisles, picking up the items I need. In the supermarket, there are too many aisles for me to do this, and I often have to ask where to find items such as olive oil, pimientos, or yeast. Another difference is in cost. Because the local store buys smaller quantities, prices are higher. The supermarket buys groceries by the truckload and can afford to sell more cheaply. Also, they often have a number of items on sale every week. The service at my local store is friendlier. Either Mr. or Mrs. Roberts is always there with a friendly greeting, and their daughter helps out on weekends and after school. They greet me by name and we have conversations about the weather or the local news. Often I meet my neighbors shopping. At the supermarket I never meet anybody I know. So many people work there that a different person is always at the checkout counter. I shop at both stores, but I enjoy my local store more.

List the five points of comparison made in the paragraph above. Notice that each point is always discussed in the *same order*—first the local store, then the supermarket.

1. _____

2. _____

3. _____

4. _____

5. _____

COMPARISON AND CONTRAST PARAGRAPHS

When you write expanded comparison and contrast paragraphs, you will find the following transitions useful.

Comparing	*Contrasting*
both	by contrast
also	on the other hand
too	unlike
have in common	instead of
share the same	but
another likeness	another difference
another similarity	

Select one of these topics for an expanded comparison and contrast paragraph. Use the outline below to make a plan.

Two Schools	Two Religions
Two Cities	Two Wars
Two Systems of Government	Two Jobs
Two Systems of Transport	Two Pets

I. _____

   A. _____

   B. _____

II. _____

   A. _____

   B. _____

III. _____

   A. _____

   B. _____

IV. _____

   A. _____

   B. _____

Write your paragraph on a separate sheet of paper.

TOPIC SENTENCES

Topic sentences are so important that you should continue working on them. To begin with, classify the topic sentences on this page according to the type of paragraph that each would introduce most appropriately. Use the abbreviations suggested in the parentheses. There may be more than one right answer for some of these sentences.

Example (E)   Process (P)   Reason (R)
Classification (C)   Definition (D)   Comparison and Contrast (CC)

_____P_____ 1. You have to do several things to get a driver's license.
_____ 2. I am a vegetarian for a number of reasons.
_____ 3. Logistics is the art of organizing supplies.
_____ 4. There are various kinds of bridges.
_____ 5. My family needs a new car.
_____ 6. What do we mean by freedom of speech?
_____ 7. Some animals are nocturnal in their habits.
_____ 8. The word *bikini* has a strange origin.
_____ 9. Some houseplants do not need sunlight.
_____ 10. Warfare changed between the two world wars.
_____ 11. You can get rid of the mice in your apartment.
_____ 12. State and Federal governments have different roles.
_____ 13. The supermarket has some interesting new products.
_____ 14. Several kinds of heavy equipment are used in road construction.
_____ 15. Anybody can learn to take good photographs.
_____ 16. There are several kinds of insults.
_____ 17. There are many differences between day schools and boarding schools.
_____ 18. It is my favorite program for several reasons.
_____ 19. Everybody should know how to do the Heimlich maneuver.
_____ 20. The word *cool* has two distinct meanings.
_____ 21. You can preserve food by drying it.
_____ 22. There are several categories of magazines.
_____ 23. This is my infallible cure for hiccups.
_____ 24. Some pedestrians have dangerous habits.
_____ 25. Tie-dyeing is fun to learn.
_____ 26. There are advantages to crop diversification.

Review what you have learned by writing six basic paragraphs, one of each type. Select topic sentences from the exercise above and work on separate sheets of paper.

TOPIC SENTENCES

The next exercise is more difficult. For each of the topics listed, write six topic sentences, one for each kind of paragraph. You will find it helpful to use certain words or expressions for each type of topic sentence.

> **Example:** examples, several, many, some
> **Process:** how to, ways of, learn
> **Reason:** reasons, why, advantages, disadvantages
> **Classification:** kinds of, types of, sorts of, classify
> **Definition:** meaning, is, what is, origin
> **Comparison and Contrast:** compare, contrast, similar, different

The first one has been done for you.

1. helicopters

    Example: *Helicopters are invaluable in many emergencies.*

    Process: *It is not very difficult to learn to fly a helicopter.*

    Reason: *I want to become a helicopter pilot for several reasons.*

    Classification: *There are several kinds of helicopters.*

    Definition: *A helicopter is a plane with a horizontal rotor.*

    Comparison/Contrast: *Helicopters differ from conventional aircraft in several ways.*

2. food

    Example: _____

    Process: _____

    Reason: _____

    Classification: _____

    Definition: _____

    Comparison/Contrast: _____

3. first aid

    Example: _____

    Process: _____

    Reason: _____

    Classification: _____

    Definition: _____

    Comparison/Contrast: _____

Continue writing topic sentences for the six kinds of paragraphs.

4. hobbies

    Example: _____

    Process: _____

    Reason: _____

    Classification: _____

    Definition: _____

    Comparison/Contrast: _____

5. friends

    Example: _____

    Process: _____

    Reason: _____

    Classification: _____

    Definition: _____

    Comparison/Contrast _____

Select a subject that you know a lot about.

6. _____

    Example: _____

    Process: _____

    Reason: _____

    Classification: _____

    Definition: _____

    Comparison/Contrast: _____

Now use the last set of sentences you have written as topic sentences for a basic paragraph of each type. Work on separate sheets of paper.

NOUN CLAUSES

You have already worked with two kinds of subordinate clauses—adjective clauses and adverb clauses. The third kind of subordinate clause is the noun clause. **Noun clauses** take the place of nouns and, like nouns, can occur in any part of a sentence. Noun clauses begin with a subordinating conjunction or with one of these relative pronouns:

who	that	whoever
whose	which	whomever
whom	what	whatever

Study the following sentences, in which the noun clauses have been placed in parentheses.

1. They do (whatever they want.)
2. (Whoever comes in first) will win the prize.
3. We said (that we had no money.)
4. I do not understand (why the package has not arrived.)
5. (That the plant is dying) is obvious.
6. They will promote (whomever they choose.)

Notice that there is a difference between noun clauses and adjective and adverb clauses. You can eliminate an adjective or adverb clause from a sentence and still have a complete sentence. This is not always true for noun clauses. One test for a noun clause is that you can replace the clause with *it*. Test the sentences above in this way. Now place parentheses around the noun clauses in the following sentences. Use the *it* test.

1. Tigers attack whatever comes their way.
2. She always gets what she wants.
3. What he would like for his birthday is a trip to Hawaii.
4. We import what we need.
5. I know what I am doing.
6. Do you really believe that there is life on Mars?
7. At least we know where they live.
8. That something was seriously wrong was evident.
9. Why your family keeps that weird pet is a mystery.
10. My ambition was that I might visit India some day.
11. Now I understand why the tapes were erased.
12. My opinion is that he is probably lying.
13. The captain asked whether we had heard the weather report.
14. All week we thought about whom we would vote for.
15. That it can jump six feet amazes me.

NOUN CLAUSES

Review the lists of subordinating conjunctions and relative pronouns. Then fill the blanks in these sentences with noun clauses.

1. I know _____.

2. We noticed _____.

3. They saw _____.

4. _____ appears odd.

5. Her reply was _____.

6. _____ is a serious error.

7. I dreamed _____.

8. They claimed _____.

9. _____ is a fact.

10. My plan is _____.

11. _____ came in the mail.

12. This letter is to say _____.

13. They fear _____.

14. Nobody knows _____.

15. Give this book to _____.

16. _____ will not be necessary.

17. _____ seems very strange.

18. Last night we discovered _____.

19. People will say _____.

20. _____ is a real danger.

Use the following noun clauses in sentences on a separate sheet of paper.

1. that she won the contest

2. that skydiving is dangerous

3. whoever gets here first

4. what is going on

5. whether we can get the job

6. why they left town

7. whoever broke my favorite mug

8. whose dog that is

9. that it is too hot to handle

10. when the moon is full

11. that we could not afford it

12. why the milk was sour

13. whatever is right

14. what he pays the babysitter

15. where you get those ideas

FIVE-PARAGRAPH ESSAYS

Now that you know how to write expanded paragraphs, you can turn them into five-paragraph essays, or compositions, by putting each one of your supporting ideas into a separate paragraph, each with its own topic sentence. You will also have a separate paragraph for your introduction and conclusion. The following is a sample of a five-paragraph essay that supports the title with examples.

Chores I Hate

There are many things about daily life that are tiresome. Like everybody else, I have a hard time waking up in the morning. I dislike having to rush through getting dressed and eating breakfast in order to be ready to leave for school on time. I do not enjoy doing dishes although my turn does not come more than twice a week. Shoveling snow can be a tough job, especially when the snow is wet and heavy. These things are bad enough, but there are three chores that I really dread above all others. They are emptying the garbage, cleaning out the fireplace, and raking leaves.

There are several things I dislike about emptying the garbage. First, by the time I get to it, the liner bag has generally been overfilled, and I have to pick it up and put it inside a full-sized plastic bag. The garbage bag is heavy, and often some sharp object like the edge of a tin can manages to poke its way through the plastic. If this happens before I get outside the house, there is more mess for me to clean up. Our garbage cans are the metal kind that tend to stick, but somehow I yank the lid off. Then, hoping the whole thing does not come apart, I heave the bag up over the rim and into the can. Last, I have to go back to the kitchen, rinse out the smelly plastic bin, and put a new liner in it.

Then there is the job of emptying the ashes out of the fireplace. Fortunately this has to be done only in the winter. I start by getting the bucket, the shovel, and the brush from the basement. I remove the firescreen, push the grate to one side, and start scraping with the shovel. This shoveling makes an ugly rasping sound, worse than chalk on a chalkboard, and raises enough dust to start me coughing. Next I have to brush out the smaller ashes that are left, creating even more dust. I have to take the bucket out of the house without touching anything because by now my hands are grimy. Then I have to carry it all the way to the compost pile on the side of the vegetable garden. Last, I have to go back, wash up, and put everything away.

Those chores are bad enough, but they are nothing compared to the annual leaf raking that goes on for days. We have an unusually large yard with about ten big maple trees and a couple of oaks. Raking the leaves seems to take all my free time after school and to ruin at least three weekends as well. I wish we could burn the leaves, but they have to be raked onto an old bedspread and dragged off to the compost pile. When it is dry enough to rake, it always seems to be windy, and my piles of leaves disappear before I can carry them away. The oak trees keep their leaves until early spring, so that I have to start all over again in March.

These three chores, emptying the trash, cleaning out the fireplace, and raking the leaves, are certainly the bane of my life, and even worse, I know that I will have to go on doing them for a number of years. I look forward to the day when I have my own family and can delegate these tasks to my children, just as soon as they are old enough. My other plan is to become an inventor and invent machines that will do these jobs.

INTRODUCTORY AND CONCLUDING PARAGRAPHS

In a five-paragraph essay, the two most difficult paragraphs to write are the introduction and the conclusion.

The introductory paragraph has three parts: introductory remarks, a thesis statement, and a plan.

Here is the first paragraph taken from the essay on the previous pages.

> There are many things about daily life that are tiresome. Like everybody else, I have a hard time waking up in the morning. I dislike having to rush through getting dressed and eating breakfast in order to be ready to leave for school on time. I do not enjoy doing dishes although my turn does not come more than twice a week. Shoveling snow can be a tough job, especially when the snow is wet and heavy. <u>These things are bad enough, but there are three chores that I really dread above all the others.</u> They are emptying the garbage, cleaning out the fireplace, and raking leaves.

The **thesis statement** has been underlined for you. In an essay the sentence that gives the main idea is called the thesis statement. The thesis statement is the most important sentence in an essay, and you always need to give it careful thought.

Everything before the thesis statement consists of **introductory remarks.** These sentences are supposed to attract the attention of your readers and arouse their interest.

Everything after the thesis statement is the **plan.** The plan lists the supporting ideas that will be introduced in the next three paragraphs. Notice that they are in order.

Next come the three supporting paragraphs, each with its own topic sentence. Turn back to the essay and underline the topic sentence in each paragraph.

The final paragraph in an essay is particularly important. It can have two parts: a summary and a conclusion.

The **summary** repeats briefly, or sums up, the ideas in the essay. You do not always need a summary; in fact, in a short essay a summary can be boring as it just repeats what has already been said in the introduction and in the supporting paragraphs. Turn back and underline the first sentence in the final paragraph of the essay. That is the summary.

The part you did not underline is called the **conclusion.** The conclusion is often the most interesting and challenging part of the essay to write. You should try to make some final comment about what you have written. It is often difficult to think of a conclusion ahead of time. While you are writing an essay, an idea for a good conclusion may just come to you. If not, you can try the suggestions on page 57.

EXAMPLE ESSAYS

Make a plan for an example essay below. Devise a topic of your own, or use one of the following. Write your essay on separate sheets of paper.

Things I Dislike about School   A Wonderful Neighborhood
Fun at the Beach   Three Treasured Possessions

Introduction

Introductory remarks: _____

_____

Thesis statement: _____

_____

Plan: _____

_____

First supporting paragraph

Topic sentence: _____

Supporting ideas: _____

_____

Second supporting paragraph

Topic sentence: _____

Supporting ideas: _____

_____

Third supporting paragraph

Topic sentence: _____

Supporting ideas: _____

_____

Conclusion

Summary*: _____

_____

Conclusion: _____

_____

*You may not need the summary, especially if you have thought of a really interesting conclusion.

INTRODUCTORY REMARKS

You can write essays of any type: example, process, reason, classification, definition, or comparison and contrast. You can write about any subject that interests you, or you can use any of the topics in this book. Your essays must always have an introduction and a conclusion, and you need at least two, and probably three, supporting paragraphs in between.

Always, once you have planned the first paragraph, you are on your way. Sometimes it is difficult to think of initial introductory remarks. Here are some suggestions to help you.

1. *A question*
   Would you like to learn to catch trout?
   Have you ever wondered what it would be like to be caught in a tornado?
   Have you ever wished you did not have to go to school?
   What was life like in America two hundred years ago?
   Do you believe in ghosts?
   How do animals survive in the desert?

2. *An explanation of why the subject is important to the reader*
   Knowing the Heimlich maneuver may enable you to save a life.
   You can make some wonderful gifts that cost almost nothing.
   You can lose weight without dieting.
   Anyone can learn to have a better memory.
   You can do several things to make a good impression when you interview for a job.

3. *A statement that is opposite of the point you plan to make*
   Many people believe that anything you buy in a health food store is good for you. (Your essay will argue that this is not the case.)
   Being a member of a large family must be wonderful. (You have a different point of view.)
   Skateboarding looks easy. (It may *look* easy, but that is all.)
   The minimum wage is quite high enough. (You will disagree.)
   There is nothing wrong with hitchhiking. (You know otherwise.)

4. *A proverb, a slogan, a saying, or a quotation*
   Many hands make light work.
   Don't count your chickens before they're hatched.
   President Truman said, "If you can't stand the heat, get out of the kitchen."
   Whatever is worth doing at all is worth doing well.
   Tall oaks from little acorns grow.

5. *A general statement*
   Probably the simplest way to begin is to discuss your subject in general and then narrow it down to the specific aspect or incident that you wish to discuss. For example, the essay about chores begins by discussing tiresome aspects of life in general and then narrows the subject down to three specific chores.

INTRODUCTORY PARAGRAPHS

Using the techniques just explained, write five introductory paragraphs. If you need more space, use a separate sheet of paper.

1. A question

_____

_____

_____

_____

2. An explanation of why the subject is important to the reader

_____

_____

_____

_____

3. A statement that is the opposite of the point you plan to make

_____

_____

_____

_____

4. A proverb, a saying, or a quotation

_____

_____

_____

_____

5. A general statement

_____

_____

_____

_____

Write a full-length essay using the best of the introductory paragraphs you have written.

CONCLUDING PARAGRAPHS

When you write an essay, you need an ending; you cannot just stop writing. You do not want the reader to turn the page looking for an ending or to wonder whether there is a page missing. A conclusion explains the significance of your writing and prevents the reader from thinking, "So what?" Often, as you write, an idea will come to you; if not, however, the following suggestions may provide inspiration.

1. *What you have learned*
   Working at a car wash is a terrible job.
   A shortcut is not always the shortest way.
   Lying can certainly get a person into trouble.
   Never again will I go camping without the proper equipment.

2. *Advice (what the reader can learn)*
   You do not always save money by buying the cheapest product.
   If you are interested in collecting coins, this is the book for you.
   Smoking is habit forming; it is best not to start.
   It is safer to walk than to accept rides from strangers.

3. *Time or place*
   It often took the pioneers months of arduous travel to cross the continent.
   When I have a family of my own, things will be different.
   In some parts of the world, people are starving.
   I certainly look forward to turning sixteen.
   In Russia students go to school for ten years instead of twelve.
   Before the industrial revolution, there was almost no air pollution.
   A hundred years from now, schools will be very different.

Write two sentences of your own for each category.

1. What you have learned

   _____

   _____

2. Advice

   _____

   _____

3. Time or **place**

   _____

   _____

RUN-ON SENTENCES

You have already learned two ways of correcting run-on sentences—you can make two sentences or you can make a compound sentence. Now that you have mastered complex sentences, you are ready to learn the third way of correcting a run-on sentence. You can often turn a run-on sentence into a complex sentence by making one of the clauses into a subordinate clause. Study the following examples and place parentheses around the subordinate clause in the corrected versions. The first one has been done for you.

1. We caught a fish it must have weighed twenty pounds.

   We caught a fish (that must have weighed twenty pounds.)

2. That plant is losing its leaves it looks dead.

   The plant that is losing its leaves looks dead.

3. The boat landed on the island coconut palms grew there.

   The boat landed on the island where coconut palms grew.

4. Return this book to the librarian she is in charge.

   Return this book to the librarian who is in charge.

5. The raccoon comes to our garbage can it has one leg missing.

   The raccoon that comes to our garbage can has one leg missing.

6. You should study physics you are very good at math.

   You should study physics because you are very good at math.

7. A man came running up to the gate the plane was taking off.

   A man came running up to the gate as the plane was taking off.

8. She wrote that book she was in her eighties.

   When she wrote that book, she was in her eighties.

9. I go to the hardware store I find something useful.

   Whenever I go to the hardware store, I find something useful.

10. The bus driver waited for me she was already late.

    The bus driver waited for me although she was already late.

In the exercise above, the first five sentences contain adjective clauses; draw an arrow to the noun the clause modifies. The last five sentences contain adverb clauses; draw an arrow to the verb each modifies.

RUN-ON SENTENCES

Correct the following run-on sentences by turning each one into a complex sentence.

1. Under the woodpile we saw a large snake it scared us.

   _____

2. We have hired a new chef he used to work in a hotel.

   _____

3. You cannot swim here the water is not safe.

   _____

4. We reached the summit it began to rain.

   _____

5. The snow fell in the night it made travel difficult.

   _____

6. I opened the windows and the doors the breeze blew through the house.

   _____

7. You broke the television you will have to pay for the repairs.

   _____

8. The forest was blackened it had burned last summer.

   _____

9. The game ended in a tie the teams had to go into overtime.

   _____

10. I found an old car it had no engine or tires.

    _____

11. Our neighbors leave town on weekends I feed their cats.

    _____

12. The poster hangs in my room it is a picture by Van Gogh.

    _____

COMBINING SENTENCES

Combine the following short sentences by turning them into either compound sentences or complex sentences. If the two ideas are of equal importance, write a compound sentence. If one of the ideas is more important than the other, write a complex sentence; place the more important idea in the main clause and the less important idea in the subordinate clause. Write your sentences on a separate sheet of paper.

1. She called the fire department. She needed help quickly.

2. I lost my favorite sweater. I had had it for years.

3. I had to stop jogging. I injured one of my knees.

4. She never has time to cook at home. She eats out a lot.

5. Turn up the heat. It is freezing in here.

6. We were exhausted from climbing all day. We kept going.

7. I ordered spaghetti. The waiter brought me chicken.

8. The algebra teacher gave us too much homework. We complained.

9. That fire will never start. You have to use more kindling.

10. We ran out of gas. We were five miles from the nearest town.

11. He lost his job. He earned money cutting firewood.

12. I have to go to the dentist next week. It is a visit I dread.

13. They attended the meeting. It was held in the firehouse.

14. That water is polluted. It is not fit to drink.

15. The traffic on that street moves fast. It is really dangerous to try to cross.

16. The sun came out. A rainbow appeared above the mountain.

17. Sally Ride was the first American woman is space. She studied astrophysics in college.

18. We sowed the corn too early. None of it came up.

19. You should not hike alone here. If you were to get hurt, nobody would ever find you.

20. My watch stopped working. I bought a new battery.

21. I turned on the air conditioner. The lights went out.

22. You should see a doctor. That rash is getting worse.

23. Some people enjoy abstract art. Others prefer more realistic work.

24. That oak tree is thirty feet tall. My parents planted it the year that I was born.